GREATER MEKONG SUBREGION GENDER STRATEGY

DECEMBER 2022

GMS SECRETARIAT
Southeast Asia Department
Asian Development Bank
6 ADB Avenue, Mandaluyong City
1550 Metro Manila, Philippines
Fax: +63 2 8636 2226
Email: gms@adb.org

Web addresses:
www.adb.org/countries/gms/main
www.greatermekong.org/

Contents

Figures

Abbreviations

ADB   Asian Development Bank

GMS-2030   GMS Economic Cooperation Program Strategic Framework 2030

GMS   Greater Mekong Subregion

RIF   GMS Regional investment Framework

SDG   Sustainable Development Goal

SEZ   special economic zone

UN   United Nations

Executive Summary

The Greater Mekong Subregion (GMS) Economic Cooperation Program is a regional cooperation platform. Established in 1992, it comprises the Kingdom of Cambodia, the People's Republic of China, the Lao People's Democratic Republic, the Republic of the Union of Myanmar, the Kingdom of Thailand, and the Socialist Republic of Viet Nam. The program supports and complements national development strategies and benefits the populations of GMS countries.

Significant achievements in regional integration and establishment of economic corridors have occurred under the GMS Program against a background of strong economic growth. Recently, the GMS Program has provided a sound basis for cooperation on responding to coronavirus disease (COVID-19) challenges.

A new GMS Economic Cooperation Strategic Framework 2030 (GMS-2030) will support enhanced regional cooperation and promote equitable sharing of the benefits of regional integration as the region begins to rebuild after the COVID-19 pandemic. If the benefits of regional integration are to be shared more equally, gender equality needs to be a focus. Gender equality is intrinsically linked to development, prosperity, and sustainability. Without the equal participation of men and women there can be no sustainability or inclusive growth. This GMS Gender Strategy is designed to support the GMS-2030 ambition of equitable sharing of benefits, by identifying opportunities to advance gender equality in GMS program activities.

A regional approach to advance gender equality in the GMS would support the efforts of individual countries on gender equality. While all GMS countries have made progress toward gender equality, and many have adopted their own national gender strategies, gender inequalities persist in the subregion. Despite significant progress in the provision of health infrastructure, high infant mortality rates and maternal mortality ratios, lack of access to health and family planning services, and high rates of gender-based violence continue. Social norms across the region continue to assign the domestic roles of caring for children and household management to women and technical work or formal employment to men. These norms have multiple and compounding effects. A GMS gender assessment was developed to provide inputs to this gender strategy. This revealed gender gaps in education attainment and overrepresentation of women in the informal sector for employment. Maternal mortality ratios and child mortality rates are high in several countries, indicating gaps in access to health care for women. The assessment found that gender inequalities were compounded by other social categorizations, including, but not limited to, disability, age, location (rural or urban), or sexual orientation.

There are a number of common challenges across the GMS that prevent individuals from fully benefiting from economic opportunities. These reduce not only national but regional economic growth and prosperity. The GMS Program, as an open platform, provides an ideal forum for GMS countries and other stakeholders, including development partners, to share experiences on gender-responsive practices and policies and develop new regional initiatives.

The objectives of the strategy are to:

(i)   improve existing methods and develop new and innovative approaches to gender mainstreaming activities to ensure equal access and participation in opportunities arising from the GMS Program;

(ii)   complement subregional efforts to explicitly address gender-based barriers affecting the full participation of individuals of all ages, abilities, and in all socioeconomic spheres; and

(iii)   address pervasive gender norms that disadvantage one group over another.

Pursuing these objectives, the GMS Gender Strategy identifies entry points for gender mainstreaming at three differentiated levels: cross-cutting themes, sectors, and projects; following the categories set under the GMS-2030.

Cross-cutting themes. The strategy identifies the following themes: macroeconomic coordination, labor mobility and safe migration, education and skills, special economic zones, and digitalization. Gender-based violence is also included as a cross-cutting theme, acknowledging the significant barrier such violence poses to full economic and social participation of women in GMS countries.

The cross-cutting themes will be adopted across the pillars set under the GMS-2030: community, connectivity, and competitiveness.

Community. The GMS Program will promote specific interventions to enhance the gender responsiveness of health services. The program will also facilitate knowledge sharing and support gender-responsive approaches to managing transmission risks and the treatment of diseases, including COVID-19. Regional action to promote environmental sustainability and address climate change will promote the participation of women in regional decision-making committees and provide avenues for training women.

Connectivity. The GMS Program will promote gender-sensitive transport and energy infrastructure through participatory consultations and gender-responsive design features. Particular emphasis will be placed on connecting more people to opportunities in economic corridors, as advancing gender equality also strengthens regional integration. The program will support technical training to increase women's employment opportunities in these sectors, carry out

awareness raising campaigns, and undertake initiatives to increase micro-, small, and medium-sized enterprises led by women.

Competitiveness. The GMS Program will promote the development of gender assessments to meet the needs of women traders and support them to scale-up their businesses through thematic training, workshops, and networking activities. Training will be provided for women working in the agriculture sector and in agri-business value chains to increase their formal participation and engagement in decision-making processes. For tourism and urban development, the GMS Program will support activities to increase women's skills and qualifications, leadership, and entrepreneurship.

The GMS Regional Investment Framework, as a centerpiece of the GMS program, will include a focus on gender equality in its prioritization of projects.

To implement the GMS Gender Strategy, opportunities to advance gender equality in ways that drive transformative change will be promoted through the collaborative mechanisms that the GMS program has successfully harnessed to date. These include: (i) policy dialogue at thematic forums and roundtables, sector forums with GMS working groups, and through the proposed establishment of a GMS task force on gender; (ii) capacity building; (iii) knowledge products; and (iv) pilot projects. These mechanisms will be enhanced through partnerships with the private sector and development partners. Gender indicators will be included in the GMS-2030 results framework, ensuring integration of gender equality across the GMS Program. A list of possible indicators is provided in the appendix of this strategy.

I. Introduction

1.   The Greater Mekong Subregion (GMS) Economic Cooperation Program Strategic Framework 2030 (GMS-2030) sets a new direction for deepening cooperation in the GMS over the next decade. It identified shared regional challenges and provided a framework to coordinate and align individual country efforts. Within this framework, gender equality is an integral cross-cutting theme across three pillars: community, connectivity, and competitiveness. The GMS-2030 vision to develop a more integrated, prosperous, sustainable, and inclusive subregion reflects the commitment by GMS countries to the United Nations (UN) Sustainable Development Goals and the Paris Agreement for Climate Change.[1]

2.   The GMS Gender Strategy supports the implementation of GMS-2030 and complements the efforts of individual countries to enhance gender equality. Leveraging the regional platform of the GMS will not only coordinate national efforts on gender equality but will add a further boost to commitments to accelerate gender equality progress across the subregion.

3.   The coronavirus disease (COVID-19) pandemic is projected to increase gender inequality and poverty in the region.[2] Traditional approaches to gender mainstreaming activities (as well as traditional strategies for economic growth) will not be sufficient to protect and expand the already substantial regional achievements in poverty reduction and gender equality. UN Women reports that women in Asia and the Pacific are more likely to have lost work due to the pandemic than men, and in some sectors, they lost jobs at twice the rate of men.[3] Unpaid care work has increased as women have taken on the task of caring for children out of school, and for family members who are ill. The incidence of domestic violence has increased, as has maternal and infant mortality.[4] A strategic focus is necessary to ensure that existing gender inequalities are not exacerbated and that women of the GMS countries are not left even further behind as a result of the pandemic.

4.   The GMS Gender Strategy supports national legislation and is based on the findings of the GMS gender assessment.[5] It outlines key strategic directions and entry points to mainstream gender across GMS investments in the sub-region. The strategy has been designed so it can be implemented flexibly and tailored at the project level to respond to evolving national gender equality regulatory frameworks, policies, and/or practices in the GMS countries. The emphasis can range from a specific focus on women and girls' empowerment, to the recognition of intersectionality as analytical framework to capture multiple dimensions of discrimination and vulnerability, including gender, age, socioeconomic status, and expanded definitions of gender discrimination that encompass men and women, as well as people whose gender identity differs from their sex assigned at birth.[6]

---

[1]   ADB. 2021. The Greater Mekong Subregion Economic Cooperation Program Strategic Framework 2030. For endorsement at the 7th GMS Summit of Leaders.

[2]   R. Carvalho and E. Lopez. 2020. Asian Women Pay the Price of the Pandemic. *South China Morning Post.* 12 December.

[3]   UN Women. 2019. *Unlocking the Lockdown: The Gendered Effects of COVID-19 on Achieving the SDGS in Asia and the Pacific.* UN Women Data Hub.

[4]   B. Susantono and A. Bhatia. 2021. A Better Normal for Women and Girls After COVID-19. ADB. Manila. 6 January.

[5]   The GMS gender assessment was an analysis of gender equality and women's situation in the GMS countries carried out through a desk review of international and national data, and an assessment of a selection of GMS projects through a gender lens. The gender assessment was a key input to the formulation of the GMS Gender Strategy.

[6]   Government of Thailand. 2015. Thailand Gender Equality Act B. E. 2558.

II. Rationale

5.   The GMS Program has delivered significant infrastructure in the GMS countries across the subregion. Regional economic corridors have facilitated mass mobility of people and goods, connected countries in new ways, contributed to their economic development, and established new shared hubs of economic activity.

6.   However, the GMS gender assessment noted that the subregion has not yet benefited from the full and equal participation of women across all social and economic spheres, nor have women benefited equally from the development achievements and efforts to date.[7] With new and innovative economic recovery strategies and investments that deliver growth, changing trade routes, and the restoration of disrupted supply chains in the post-COVID-19 period, it is timely to revisit the economic uplift that greater gender equality can provide.

7.   The GMS Gender Strategy will support individual country efforts by strengthening gender mainstreaming activities in GMS operations and leveraging its regional collaborative platform to aggregate efforts on gender equality, share learning, and explore joint or bilateral opportunities. A regional approach to gender mainstreaming in the GMS is needed for the following reasons.

> Despite the good progress that has been achieved, gender inequality persists across the GMS.

8.   GMS countries have made good progress toward gender equality since 2000. According to the Gender Inequality Index of the United Nations Development Program (UNDP), in 2020, all GMS countries improved or maintained their rankings.[8] Out of 189 economies, the People's Republic of China (PRC) was ranked 39th, Viet Nam 65th, Thailand 80th, the Lao People's Democratic Republic (Lao PDR) 113rd, Cambodia 117th, and Myanmar 118th in 2020.

9.   Although all GMS countries have adopted country-specific strategies to achieve Sustainable Development Goal (SDG) 5 on gender equality, persistent issues with gendered impacts remain. These include high infant and maternal mortality, early marriage (before the age of 18), gender-based violence, and low formal sector employment. Deforestation and climate-related environmental change also disproportionately affect women, particularly rural women. A renewed effort is needed to prevent and manage these impacts and advance gender equality in the subregion.

---

[7]   ADB. GMS Gender Assessment. Unpublished.

[8]   The gender inequality index measures (i) human development through statistics on maternal mortality and adolescent birth rates, (ii) empowerment based on the proportion of women in parliament and of men and women over the age of 25 with secondary educations, and (iii) economic status measured by labor force participation rate of men and women over 15 years of age. Data included in this report were obtained in 2019. UNDP. 2020. *Human Development Report. The Next Frontier – Human Development and the Anthropocene.* New York.

10. The GMS gender assessment identified gender norms as a significant barrier to women's full integration and participation in society. These norms limit life opportunities and contribute to gender inequality. Lack of access to health and family planning services, gender-based violence, and occupational segregation, together with the assignment of functions that include child rearing, household duties, and caring for sick and elderly family members to women mean that men hold higher paid jobs and take more decision-making roles in public life. While many people are highly entrepreneurial, women have limited access to financial services, lower digital literacy, and less access to digital technologies. They work overwhelmingly in the informal economy. In most GMS countries, men are the head of the household, notwithstanding individual household personal dynamics. These norms not only constrain women's autonomy and equality, but they also deprive the economy of their potential contribution to economic growth and prosperity. Increasing women's participation in the economy is consistently identified as a basic element in boosting economic growth.

11. Although the GMS gender assessment found that the gender gap had continued to close slowly over the past 10 years, there are opportunities to accelerate these through a concerted joint effort that uses the GMS Program as an open platform.[9] The GMS gender strategy will support a range of laws and policies that are already in place to support gender equality and women's empowerment.

> COVID-19 has exacerbated existing inequalities, especially gender disparities, and, if these are not addressed, hard-fought gains for equality in the subregion will be lost.

12. Women have been on the frontline of COVID-19 response efforts. They not only make up the majority of health workers in all GMS countries but also of informal carers due to gender norms.[10] Women and girls bear the burden of caring for sick and vulnerable family members and implementing COVID-19-safe household practices.

13. The pandemic has deepened pre-existing inequalities for women as a result of the gender pay gap and the often-precarious nature of women's jobs; women's unpaid care burden, which has been increased by school closures and family illnesses; an increase in gender-based violence due to "lockdown" measures; and mobility restrictions that have reduced access to health care, including reproductive health care.[11]

14. Restrictions on mobility have also increased the time people in the GMS have spent on digital platforms. This increases the risks for vulnerable users from online predatory activity. Higher levels of gendered online abuse have been reported.[12] Barriers to education access and achievement have been intensified as participation has been disrupted and individuals have been forced to shelter at home during public health lockdowns.

---

[9]   The GMS-2030 aims to reform the GMS Program to be a more open platform that cooperates closely with other regional cooperation and integration initiatives while encouraging diverse stakeholders from central and local governments, private and public sectors, academia, civil society, and development partners to actively participate in the Program's operations.

[10] M. Boniol et al. 2019. Gender Equity in the Health Workforce: Analysis of 104 Countries. *Health Workforce Working Paper* 1. Geneva: World Health Organization. March.

[11] E. Hill and M. Baird. 2020. COVID-19, Economic Crisis and Gender Equality in Asia 2020. *East Asia Forum*. 10 June.

[12] Plan International, Save The Children (2020). Because We Matter: Addressing COVID-19 and Violence Against Girls in Asia-Pacfic.

[13] J. Woetze et al. 2018. *The Power of Parity: Advancing Women's Equality in Asia Pacific.* McKinsey Global Institute. 23 April.

[14] A. Madgavkar et al. 2020. *COVID-19 and Gender Equality: Countering the Regressive Effects.* McKinsey Global Institute. 15 July.

15.   Prior to the outbreak of the COVID-19 pandemic, McKinsey estimated that tackling gender inequality in the Asia and Pacific region would increase gross domestic product (GDP) by 12% by 2025 under a business-as-usual scenario.[13] As a result of COVID-19, global GDP is now expected to suffer a $1 trillion loss.[14]

> The GMS Program, as an open platform, provides an ideal forum for GMS countries to share experiences and bring in development partners' gender expertise.

16.   Each GMS country is committed to advancing gender equality and to achieving the transformative agenda of SDG 5 on gender equality. There are many shared challenges that cross borders or affect citizens of many countries in the region, so it makes sense to combine efforts. Sharing of knowledge and experience on good practices and lessons learned can strengthen individual national gender mainstreaming and equality measures, as well as regional actions.

17.   Likewise, the GMS development partners are committed to advancing gender equality and already work in cooperation with GMS countries as well as across country borders. A regional approach to gender equality will not only give visible support for inclusion in GMS activities, but can harness the joint efforts of GMS countries and financing partners, through strategic placement in investment projects.

18.   The open platform of the GMS provides a good forum for dialogue and collaboration on gender equality knowledge sharing and to develop new initiatives. It will help improve targeting of development efforts across the region and support new strategic alliances with other entities.

---

[14]   A. Madgavkar et al. 2020. *COVID-19 and Gender Equality: Countering the Regressive Effects.* McKinsey Global Institute. 15 July.

III. Approach and Objectives

19. Innovative approaches, together with traditional interventions that deliver sustainable gender equality outcomes, are needed if the economic and social gains made in recent years are to be preserved, particularly following the COVID-19 pandemic. They can lay a foundation for greater achievements in gender equality in the future.

20. The GMS Gender Strategy positions gender within each of the three pillars of the GMS-2030: community, connectivity, and competitiveness. Identifying common regional gender equality challenges, the strategy includes both specific and integrated approaches for advancing gender equality and the empowerment of women across the subregion. It is designed to complement the national strategies on gender of GMS countries and their individual efforts to achieve gender equality.

21. While the strategy provides a simple framework of entry points in projects to address gender equality across the breadth of GMS projects, it also harnesses the strength of the GMS Program as a platform for regional collective activities which have sub-national, national, and regional impact.

22. The strategy will also provide a focus for the transformative work of shifting gender norms that entrench gender inequality. The strategy focuses on making gender visible in all the stages of GMS projects and programs: investment planning, conception, prioritization, design, implementation, administration, and evaluation. Informed by the GMS gender assessment, the strategy draws on best practices, including from development partners, to stimulate innovation in regional gender mainstreaming activities. The GMS Gender Strategy aims to leverage the subregional engagement platform of the GMS to achieve three objectives (Figure 1).

23. This strategy provides a gender lens that can be cast across GMS program activities to reveal the influence of hidden gender biases or assumptions, identify entry points to advance gender equality, and address intersectional impacts, such as age, disability, ethnicity, and remote geographic location that amplify gender inequality in the subregion.

Figure 1: Objectives of the Greater Mekong Subregion Gender Strategy

Objective 1
Improve existing methods and develop new and innovative approaches to gender mainstreaming activities to ensure equal access and participation in opportunities arising from the GMS Program.

Objective 2
Complement subregional efforts to explicitly address barriers affecting the full participation of women and men of all ages and abilities in all socioeconomic spheres.[a]

Objective 3
Address pervasive gender norms that disadvantage one group over another.

ASEAN = Association of Southeast Asian Nations, GMS = Greater Mekong Subregion.

[a] Including the ASEAN Declaration on the Gender Responsive Coordination and Implementation of the ASEAN Community Vision 2025 and the Sustainable Development Goals; ASEAN Regional Plan of Action on Ending Violence Against Women 2016–2025; and ASEAN Regional Plan of Action on Women, Peace and Security in ASEAN.

Source: The GMS Secretariat.

IV. Key Gender Entry Points

24. The economic and social benefits of increased regional and intraregional connectivity, as well as improved regional competitiveness should be enjoyed by every person living in the GMS countries. The GMS gender assessment revealed there are gaps and also barriers to participation and access to the benefits that flow from regional cooperation. Social norms that assign individuals to specific gender roles have been slow to shift. Gender gaps in participation and attainment in education, including in vocational education and training; gender segregation in the formal and informal economy; unequal access to health care; and high rates of gender-based violence—all these highlight that more can be done to improve participation in the economic growth of the region, remove barriers to accessing services and the labor market, and enable more people to share in the advantages that regional integration can deliver.

25. Fundamental shifts and realignments are occurring across many economic sectors. Some jobs have been lost forever, while in other sectors, workers have moved to take up new opportunities that have emerged as a result of the pandemic, and which e-commerce has accelerated, potentially exacerbating the digital gender gap.[15] The extent of the care economy has also been revealed, as public health responses during the pandemic have laid bare the extent of women's labor in the informal care economy at home, and the formal care economy in the highly gender-segregated health workforce. Addressing these issues and tackling underpinning gender norms and attitudes will be critical to supporting the success of the gender equality strategy across the region.

26. The availability of robust sex-disaggregated data sets plays an important role in informing policy makers. Compiling such data is an important first step in addressing impacts. Targeting policy and program responses has been hampered by the lack of sex-disaggregated data across the region. Ensuring this data is collected in GMS program activities will enhance evidence-based gender-responsive policy making.

27. All these challenges are linked. The GMS Gender Strategy proposes to address them through the traditional GMS program approach of thematic sectors, which are shown in Figure 2, and to incorporate new areas as cross-cutting themes across these sectors. Incorporating macroeconomic cooperation to coordinate efforts to address, for example, the impacts of the pandemic and to stabilize supply chains, cooperation on labor mobility and migration, digitization, special economic zones, and education will deepen and add additional value to regional collaboration efforts. Assessment of priority projects under the Regional Investment Framework (RIF) will also incorporate a gender equality element. All these will embed gender mainstreaming in the GMS program in a more comprehensive way.

28. The activities and concepts described below are deliberately flexible. The aim is to promote innovative new responses to new areas of work and established pillars where gains are still to be made. The socioeconomic and cultural diversity of the GMS countries means that the following recommendations will need to be adapted and refined for each country context.

---

[15]   D. Roland-Holst and S. Westover. 2021. *COVID-19 Food Security Response and Recovery Actions in the GMS*. Manila: ADB and GMS.

Figure 2: Pillars and Other Thematic Areas of the Greater Mekong Subregion

GMS - 2030

COMMUNITY	CONNECTIVITY	COMPETITIVENESS
• Health Cooperation • Environmental Sustainability and Climate Change	• Transport • Energy	• Trade and Investment • Agriculture • Tourism • Urban Development

Other areas: SDGs, ICTs, e-commerce, logistics, labor mobility and safe migration, education and skills, special economic zones, development partner and private sector participation.

GMS-2030 = Greater Mekong Subregion Economic Cooperation Program Strategic Framework 2030, ICT = information and communication technology, SDG = Sustainable Development Goal.

Source: The GMS Secretariat.

A. Cross-Cutting Themes

29. The GMS-2030 outlines emerging or new areas for cooperation under the GMS program. These areas are specific multi-sector or cross-cutting topics that boost the value of the GMS thematic sector activities. In addition to key strategic entry points to mainstream gender across these emerging new areas, this section refers to actions to promote inclusion and change attitudes to discriminatory gender norms.

30. The GMS gender assessment noted that regional integration benefits were not shared equally, and that gender is a factor in this unequal distribution. A "gender lens" helps reveal groups who may not be participating in or benefiting from GMS activities. It also provides an entry point to deepen the impact of GMS activities by incorporating gender-responsive actions that take into account women's care burden and gender discrimination, ensuring that GMS program activities have a greater impact.

31. The gender assessment also found:

(a) that gender-based violence is pervasive in the region, and action is required to shift norms and attitudes that normalize violence within the family setting or based on gender; and

(b) there is significant unmet demand for reproductive health care for certain groups.

32. Regional integration or trade programs do not traditionally address social issues that operate as a barrier to economic participation. However, the GMS platform is focused on sharing the benefits of regional integration and supporting an inclusive subregion, cross-cutting themes that can be used to address clear gender gaps in the subregion.

(i) Macroeconomic Coordination

33. Macroeconomic policy is often considered to be gender neutral. However, fiscal and monetary policies impact women differently than men. Typically, women work in service-oriented sectors; they have lower salaries, even for work of equal value across the subregion, and have limited access to resources and physical assets to manage economic shocks.

34. The COVID-19 pandemic has required significant unplanned government expenditure to ameliorate the situation for the poorest and most vulnerable people and industries, including for businesses and health care providers. New tax policies or reductions in spending, particularly social spending, are typical tools used to manage unforeseen budget pressures.[16] Far more women than men use services such as social assistance, health, school, and community support. Monetary and trade policies, whether expansive or restrictive, are also used to manage domestic priorities.

35. The GMS Program will provide a platform that will enable macroeconomic coordination to be viewed through a gender lens. Gender-responsive budgeting is an area where expertise and experience within the GMS region can be shared.

---

[16]   UN Women. 2015. Why Macroeconomic Policy Matters for Gender Equality. *UN Women Policy Brief* No. 4. New York.

36. Recognizing the interconnected nature of the GMS countries, analysis of the distributional impacts of proposals on a regional basis will be promoted for regional projects. This can highlight where gaps in national policies occur and identify areas for reform and program support. Through this strategy, the program will also promote equal economic opportunities for women and other groups.

(ii) Labor Mobility and Safe Migration

37. The GMS gender assessment noted the high rates of migration in GMS countries and the vulnerability of female migrants, particularly those from ethnic minority groups and gender-diverse individuals, to exploitation and harassment.

38. The GMS Program will promote gender-responsive safe internal mobility and lifelong skills. This is relevant not only in GMS infrastructure and tourism projects, but also in manufacturing sectors characterized by migrant workforces and regional or border areas where migrant recruitment occurs. Education and training on migrants' opportunities and rights in conjunction with GMS countries and international nongovernment organizations (NGOs) will be explored.

(iii) Education and Skills

39. Significant gains in girls' education have been made across the subregion, with gender parity achieved or exceeded in some countries, notwithstanding significant gaps for girls from rural areas and from minority ethnic communities. A shared opportunity exists to build on the great gains in girls' education in the region by encouraging girls and women into higher-paid, technical, or managerial and leadership roles in the workforce.

40. The GMS Program will support the Association of Southeast Asian Nations (ASEAN) in its work in education. It will pursue the inclusion of formal technical and vocational education and training (TVET) as well as leadership education for women and girls, and networks for women in leadership or in

non-traditional roles and sectors (such as public life and the public sector, STEM education areas, defense and national security). Infrastructure investments with employment opportunities will continue to include gender targets in employment and training. The GMS Program will also promote links to local education institutions and partnerships that will include scholarships, paid internships, mentoring and shadowing programs, as well as flexible work arrangements such as part-time work and work from home, to increase the number of women in higher skilled jobs.

(iv) Special Economic Zones

41. Special economic zones (SEZs) support industry competitiveness and attract foreign and domestic investment. They also act as job hubs, often providing safer and more reliable employment opportunities than are available otherwise, especially for women. A report by the World Bank on SEZs in eight developing countries found that 60%–80% of the workforce in SEZs was female.[17]

42. Favorable taxation and regulatory regimes support business investment in SEZs. The GMS Program will support investment in equal employment opportunities at all levels in SEZs, through incorporating core labor standards in SEZ projects as well as gender-responsive human resource policies, such as child care, access to health care, part-time work and flexible working hours for all employees.

(v) Digitization and New Technologies

43. The digital revolution is a cross-cutting theme in the GMS-2030 Strategy. Digital communication has been an essential tool during the COVID-19 pandemic and has operated effectively in many circumstances to convey vital health and safety information. However, the digital gender gap in GMS countries requires determined action to identify opportunities and niches within GMS activities to ensure equitable access not only to digital technology but also to higher-level digital employment opportunities for

[17]   World Bank. 2012. *Fostering Women's Economic Empowerment through Special Economic Zones: Comparative Analysis of Eight Countries and Implications for Governments, Zone Authorities and Businesses.* Washington, DC.

women. In remote areas, addressing gender barriers in access to mobile telephones, for example, and other digital technologies can enhance access to services and community networks.

44.   The GMS Program will enhance partnerships with the private sector, NGOs, and financiers to facilitate access and connection to the use of digital technology by marginalized groups in society through financing and training programs. Similarly, the program will identify opportunities to support women in technical and leadership roles in digital technology and e-commerce and to provide pathways for entering information and communication technology fields direct from education or existing employment.

(vi) Gender Norms and Attitudes

45.   The GMS gender assessment reported on the high rates of gender-based violence in the subregion, the significant unpaid care burden of women, and gaps in access to health and education services. These all reflect gender norms and attitudes—at home, work, and within the community—that act as barriers to full participation and enjoyment of the economic and social benefits that successful regional integration supports.

46.   The GMS program will conduct its activities to promote inclusion and change attitudes to gender norms that operate to favor one group over another. It will look for opportunities, such as use of inclusive language in public communications, and gender analysis informed by an intersectional lens across GMS region programs as an important step toward a sustainable and gender-equal GMS region.

B. Sectors

47.   The GMS-2030 Strategy maps out a vision of a more integrated, prosperous, sustainable, and inclusive subregion. Utilizing the three pillars of

community, connectivity, and competitiveness, which are the fundamental strengths of the GMS program, the GMS 2030 Strategy focuses on optimization of resources and action. The Gender Strategy adopts a similar philosophy.

Pillar 1: Community

48.   Focusing on people and the region, the community pillar targets the health sector, environmental sustainability, and climate change.

(i) Health

49.   The GMS gender assessment identified an unmet demand for health care across most GMS countries, particularly for reproductive and maternal health care and family planning services. It found significant rates of teenage pregnancy, high maternal and infant mortality, and high childhood stunting rates. For women, adequate health care is the key to relief from time-consuming informal obligations to care for sick children and family members. Alleviating time poverty by reducing the burden of illness and disease improves gender equality outcomes. Gender-diverse people are more likely to experience stigma and discrimination, including from health workers, reducing their access to health services.[18]

50.   The COVID-19 pandemic has highlighted not only the gendered downstream impacts of communicable disease management, but that communicable disease transmission and management also needs to be considered from a gender perspective.[19]

51.   The GMS Program will promote specific interventions, particularly those in remote areas with ethnic minority populations or areas where migrant populations transit or congregate, to enhance access to health services for women and other marginalized groups.[20] It will explore

---

[18]   K. Blondeel et al. 2018. Violence Motivated by Perception of Sexual Orientation and Gender Identity: A Systematic Review. *Bulletin of the World Health Organization*. 96 (1). pp. 29–41L.

[19]   World Bank. 2020. Gender Dimensions of the COVID-19 Pandemic. *Policy Note*. 16 April.

[20]   Marginalized groups are people at the intersections of poverty, sex, age, disability, ethnicity, and unemployment, and are at greater disadvantage or risk of exclusion.

opportunities to share experiences and develop regional responses to increasing reproductive health care services, education and advice (with a specific focus on youth, women, and men), and institutional capacity development on the links between health and gender. Programmatic responses, including reproductive health briefing sessions for the construction workforce in gender action plans activities in GMS-financed construction projects, or for the community where projects are operating in remote or rural locations, will also be included with the support of implementing agencies and others.

52. The GMS Program will support gender-responsive approaches to managing transmission risks and treatment of communicable diseases such as COVID-19 and may consider options for knowledge sharing on managing disease burdens generally.

(ii) Environmental Sustainability and Climate Change

53. Environmental sustainability and climate change are of critical importance to women, particularly women in rural areas. Women are more likely than men to live in poverty, and it is the poor who are at greatest risk from climate shocks and environmental degradation. According to the UN, women are also particularly underrepresented in decision-making on climate change, disaster risk management, and sustainability.[21]

54. The GMS program will contribute to women's empowerment by enhancing their participation in regional decision making on natural resources, environmental management, and disaster response committees and activities. It will apply gender-sensitive approaches to adaptation and mitigation programs to reduce the impact of climate shocks and environmental degradation on women. GMS activities on climate resilience and in the natural resources and environment sector will also provide avenues for training for women, both as professionals in the sector and as ecosystem managers and decision makers.

Pillar 2: Connectivity

55. This pillar focuses on significant infrastructure investments in transport and energy, which provide products and services that enhance the way women and men live.

(i) Transport

56. Access to education, employment, health care, and markets depends on transport. Poor transport infrastructure reduces incomes, increases maternal mortality ratios, and raises the cost of food. It is also linked to lower levels of girls' enrollment in school.[22] Poorly designed road infrastructure increases fatalities for drivers, passengers, and other road users, either in vehicles or as pedestrians.

57. Investments in transport and logistics improve inter-regional and intra-regional mobility. Transport infrastructure designed to accommodate the different needs of users include "hard" measures such as wide roadside pathways and accessible overpasses, lighting to increase safety, public toilets and rest areas, and security measures to protect individuals from harassment. It also requires "soft" infrastructure such as public transport interconnections to take account of women's pattern of transport use, which often involves multiple stops for education, health and child care, market shopping, and employment in 1 day. Gender-sensitive timetabling would reduce the time women spend on travel for domestic tasks or for employment and increase their mobility. It could also facilitate access to markets for women traders.

58. The GMS program will promote gender-sensitive transport infrastructure design and provide well-lit public areas to respond to concerns for safety of movement, particularly at night. The program will work with transport and logistics operators to improve gender-sensitive customer services to enhance the utility of the infrastructure for all users. Identifying entry points for women-led businesses to supply services to infrastructure civil works or to

---

[21]   United Nations Framework Convention on Climate Change. 2020. Introduction to Gender and Climate Change.

[22]   United Nations Development Fund for Women; World Bank; ADB; United Nations Development Programme; and the Government of the United Kingdom, Department for International Development. 2004. *A Fair Share for Women: Cambodia Gender Assessment.* Phnom Penh.

be developed within or adjacent to the transport infrastructure will also be a feature of GMS projects. The GMS platform will operate as a forum to share learning and innovation on transport access and poverty-sensitive pricing policies or subsidies.

(ii) Energy

59. Investment in energy infrastructure reduces indoor air pollution and improves health outcomes for women and their children. It also frees women and girls from household drudgery by reducing the time needed for cooking and collecting fuel for cooking and heating. The time saved opens opportunities for women to integrate themselves into the formal economy through education, employment outside the home, and community decision-making activities.

60. This sector refers to energy infrastructure, powering, and delivering connections within the subregion and region. Investments in energy improve international competitiveness, support urban development, buoy trade and tourism, and advance regional cooperation and integration. Although most household energy users are women, applying a gender analysis or approach to energy infrastructure investments is not a common practice across the subregion. Improved affordability, reliability, and access to energy can minimize the burden of unpaid care work for women and enhance their capacity to develop energy-based livelihoods or income generation. Targeted actions to encourage women to participate in decision-making and employment around energy sector investments can improve the economic reach of national, subregional, and regional programs.

(iii) Gender Mainstreaming in Infrastructure

61. To boost gender mainstreaming in the transport and energy infrastructure sectors, the GMS Program will promote gender mainstreaming through participatory consultation and employment opportunities in unskilled and skilled roles in infrastructure construction projects. Business skills development training, including identifying income-

earning opportunities for local communities, will also be promoted to encourage women and men to start new businesses. The GMS will support initiatives that increase the access of women-owned micro, small, and medium-sized enterprises (MSMEs) to information on financial products to bridge the finance gap for female entrepreneurs and to enhance market access through increased mobility and reliable power sources.

62. Construction workforces are often large and itinerant and are associated with an increased risk of sexual exploitation, abuse, and harassment (SEAH).[23] The GMS Program will support awareness raising campaigns to facilitate longer-term attitudinal changes that will support gender equality, workforce, and community education. The GMS program will also facilitate training to raise awareness of SEAH and approaches to prevention, mitigation, and response measures. Working with financiers, the GMS program will respond to opportunities to implement SEAH mechanisms in specific projects, noting that initiatives should extend beyond the life of the initial project.

63. The GMS Program will pursue institutional gender mainstreaming activities, with energy utilities and with national and municipal transport entities to support institutional gender mainstreaming. These efforts will implement modern gender-equitable human resource management practices and policies.

Pillar 3: Competitiveness

64. This pillar covers trade and investment facilitation, agriculture, tourism, and urban development.

65. The COVID-19 pandemic has reduced cross-border trade and broken supply chains, including in agricultural markets. It has also halted international tourism, reduced investment flows to the region, and diminished the economic and social dynamism of urban environments. People smuggling, people trafficking, and modern slavery are expected to rise.[24]

---

[23]   World Bank. 2020. *Good Practice Note: Addressing Gender Based Violence in Investment Project Financing involving Major Civil Works.* Washington, DC.

(i) Trade and Investment Facilitation

66. Female cross-border traders often operate in informal and precarious employment channels. These channels are a significant element of cross-border trade and are estimated to account for up to 30% of all trade across borders.[25] Female-owned enterprises are associated with limited access to finance, markets and technology, and limited capacity to scale. However, women cross-border traders can be charged higher tax rates than men and can pay 100% more for transportation costs for goods than men.[26]

67. GMS trade programs will target these issues and use the convening power of the GMS to support the development of gender-responsive regional financial and business development solutions. Programs will work with the private sector, including financial institutions, on gender mainstreaming as well as women's access to finance to support the scaling up of women's businesses into new higher-value sectors.

68. The GMS Program will promote the development of gender assessments to map trade impacts and women's specific trade activities. Trade programs will include strategies to manage gendered impacts of trade, as well as gender-sensitive training. The GMS Program will support workshops on trade skills, trade networking platforms, and work with regulatory bodies to remove barriers to competitive cross-border trading for women. These measures—together with government engagement to streamline border taxation, address corruption and improve cross-border infrastructure—will improve not only the competitiveness of women's businesses but the efficiency of cross-border trade generally.

(ii) Agriculture

69. In agriculture, women are overwhelmingly clustered in the smallholding sector, farming at a micro-level, including as unpaid family laborers. Low levels of literacy and lack of knowledge of markets or access to finance limit the opportunities for women to scale up their businesses. In addition, gender norms on women's roles in the home and in agriculture can operate as further barriers to scale.

70. The GMS Program will support the extension of female-centered agriculture extension projects to help women to scale-up production. It will target support to women farmers to take up new products and services and participate in agribusiness value chains. The GMS will also support innovative programs that increase agricultural output and support changes in gender relations.[27]

71. The GMS Program, aligned with environmental sustainability and climate resilience activities under the community stream, will also promote initiatives to increase women's formal participation and decision-making roles in agricultural bodies, and in public life, including through land titling initiatives for women.

(iii) Tourism

72. The GMS gender assessment found that women accounted for the majority of workers in the tourism sector, but that they were overrepresented in informal and precarious jobs and underrepresented in management and leadership roles.

---

[24]   Government of Australia, Department of Foreign Affairs and Trade. 2020. *Partnerships for Recovery—Australia's COVID-19 Development Response*. Canberra.

[25]   C. Krainara. 2013. *Cross Border Trade Outlook in the GMS*. March.

[26]   M. Seror, R. Record, and J. Clarke. 2018. Glass Barriers: Constraints to Women's Small-Scale, Cross-Border Trade in Cambodia and Lao PDR. In *Trade and Poverty Reduction: New Evidence of Impacts in Developing Countries*. Geneva: World Bank and World Trade Organization.

[27]   For example: Australian Centre for International Agricultural Research. Gender Equitable Agricultural Extension through Institutions and Youth Engagement in Papua New Guinea, and Analysing Gender Transformative Approaches to Agricultural Development with Ethnic Minority Communities in Vietnam.

73.   The COVID-19 pandemic shut down international tourism and severely impacted regional and domestic tourism in GMS countries. In rebuilding the tourism sector from the pandemic and in ensuring a focus on sustainability and harnessing digital technology, the GMS Program will enhance access of information and work to open up more tourism employment opportunities to women and local communities, as well as promoting specific initiatives for women who participate in tourism employment cross-border migrant flows.

74.   The GMS Program will also support activities aimed at improving the skills and qualifications of women working in tourism. This strategy will enhance the inclusion of female leadership and entrepreneurship features in GMS tourism projects. Bearing in mind the risk of human trafficking, sexual exploitation, and harassment in the sector, the program will support prevention, reporting, and risk mitigation activities in tourism and civil works projects in tourism areas, including awareness raising and reporting mechanisms for human trafficking.

(iv) Urban Development

75.   Improving urban environments and infrastructure, particularly housing, water and sanitation, waste management, public lighting, and recreation facilities, will directly impact women in a positive way. Many urban environments in the GMS subregion are under pressure from population growth, often due to internal migration, and are characterized by temporary housing settlements and crowded environments. Water, sanitation, and power services are often limited, and safety and security are absent. These are all matters that impact women as domestic carers and workers.

76.   While GMS projects traditionally involve participatory consultation processes with women, girls, and other marginalized groups, women remain underrepresented in formal decision-making roles within municipal service authorities and city planning.[28] The GMS Program will promote institutional gender mainstreaming to accelerate not only the responsiveness of urban services to female

users, but to increase the percentage of the urban management workforce that is female.

77.   The GMS Program will support activities that promote women's participation and leadership in urban planning through scholarships, internships, professional mentoring, and awareness-raising activities. GMS projects will address specific challenges in urban environments, such as access and safety, including through the innovative use of technology, lighting of public spaces, and gender-sensitive and inclusive design.

(v) Bridging the Gender Gap in Regional Competitiveness

78.   To address the overall gender gap in trading sectors, the GMS Program will seek to include initiatives for female-led business startups in GMS projects in other sectors. The GMS Program will look to partner in events to increase women traders' knowledge of markets and regulatory requirements and to create partnerships with private sector partners for low or no collateral credit facilities to increase sales or connections to markets and service providers. The program will support greater access by women to e-commerce platforms to create an enabling business environment for female entrepreneurs.

C. Projects: Greater Mekong Subregion Regional Investment Framework

79.   The Regional Investment Framework (RIF) helps to identify priority infrastructure projects in the GMS. The RIF contains projects that have identified funding, others that are under implementation, and projects that are yet to be funded, as well as projects that represent possible future directions. The RIF has operated as an infrastructure overview by helping to identify alignment in regional and national planning across the GMS projects.

80.   The GMS-2030 envisages a new pipeline of projects that share the benefits of regional

---

[28]   *World Bank.* 2020. *Gender Inclusive Cities: Can Urban Planning Take Into Account Gender and Minorities?* Washington, DC.

cooperation and integration. The RIF will remain the backbone of the GMS program. Its projects will increase the competitiveness of the region and support social returns, including greater inclusion, sustainability, and gender equality. Such returns are increasingly part of development partner financing guidelines and are reflected in private sector funders' corporate social responsibility policies. Incorporating social returns such as gender equality into the assessment of RIF projects will make the RIF a powerful tool to advance gender equality in the GMS region.

81. For individual infrastructure projects to be included in the RIF, a gender assessment of the project and the extent to which it targets and closes gender gaps will be used to inform infrastructure investment prioritization decisions.

V. Implementation

82. The GMS countries will use the GMS platform to aggregate their individual efforts to accelerate gender equality. For the strategic entry points in the previous section to become a reality, the GMS Program will use different implementation mechanisms that have been proved to be successful, including: policy dialogue, capacity building, knowledge products, and pilot projects.

83. The proposed implementation mechanisms in Figure 3 will provide opportunities for development partners, civil society organizations, and the private sector to not only participate in but to partner with the GMS Program and GMS countries in taking the GMS Gender Strategy forward.

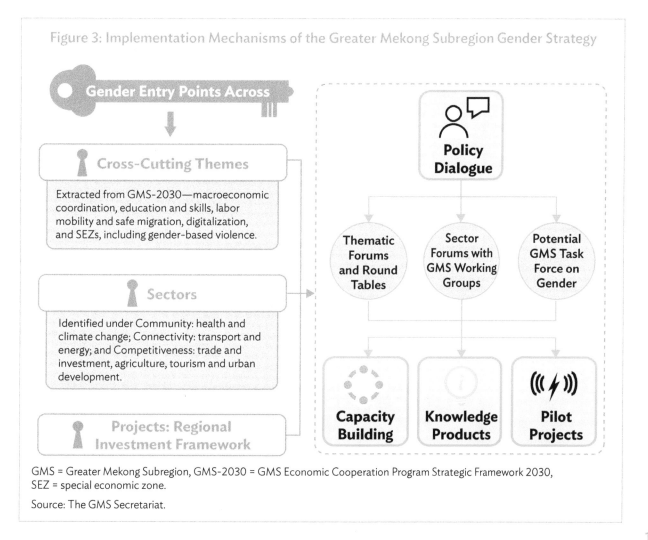

Figure 3: Implementation Mechanisms of the Greater Mekong Subregion Gender Strategy

Gender Entry Points Across

Cross-Cutting Themes

Extracted from GMS-2030—macroeconomic coordination, education and skills, labor mobility and safe migration, digitalization, and SEZs, including gender-based violence.

Sectors

Identified under Community: health and climate change; Connectivity: transport and energy; and Competitiveness: trade and investment, agriculture, tourism and urban development.

Projects: Regional Investment Framework

Policy Dialogue

Thematic Forums and Round Tables

Sector Forums with GMS Working Groups

Potential GMS Task Force on Gender

Capacity Building

Knowledge Products

Pilot Projects

GMS = Greater Mekong Subregion, GMS-2030 = GMS Economic Cooperation Program Strategic Framework 2030, SEZ = special economic zone.

Source: The GMS Secretariat.

A. Policy Dialogue

84. The GMS Program will promote policy dialogue to inform and assist countries to develop or share national expertise in gender mainstreaming across GMS activity areas. Policy dialogue will provide a platform for GMS countries with deep expertise to share lessons learned and work together to identify solutions to regional challenges. Development partners and civil society organizations' support and expertise will be a valuable contribution to this.

85. The instruments to be used for enhanced policy dialogue on gender equality may include: (i) thematic forums and round tables, (ii) sector forums with GMS working groups, and (iii) the establishment of a potential GMS task force on gender.

(i)   Thematic Forums and Round Tables

86. A series of thematic forums, exploring gender equality entry points with GMS countries and ADB project teams, will enhance regional collaboration and build a sense of community around common objectives. The GMS gender assessment highlighted the opportunity for knowledge sharing to improve the capacity of implementing agencies to deliver gender equality activities and impacts. The assessment also noted the expertise already available within GMS countries, in women's corresponding ministries or agencies and civil society. In many instances, the private sector is taking the lead on gender equality and has the expertise to contribute further in the future. GMS forums and round tables will enable participants to explore gender equality entry points in forthcoming projects, opportunities for collaboration on specific issues, and areas for further action or research.

(ii)   Sector Forums with Greater Mekong Subregion Working Groups

87. The GMS Program operates through a multi-tiered organizational structure (Figure 4) that includes a Summit of Leaders, Ministerial Conferences, and Senior Officials' Meetings, supported by nine sector working groups and four forums and councils.[29] GMS working groups have been the primary vehicle for taking forward work in specific sectors under the GMS program. With membership drawn from ranks of experts in GMS countries, the working groups develop workplans to address identified issues and report to sectoral ministerial meetings and other higher mechanisms. The GMS Gender Strategy will serve as a guide for already established and future GMS working groups to review existing sectoral workplans and priority areas through a gender lens, and to identify new entry points.

(iii)   Establishment of a Potential Greater Mekong Subregion Task Force on Gender

88. As noted in Figure 1, in some cases, task forces are created by the GMS Program for an interim period to explore the potential of a sector or working area. These task forces may or may not then be formalized into working groups if agreed by GMS countries.

89. In addition to the implementation mechanisms that have already been discussed, a GMS gender task force could be established to take the GMS Gender Strategy forward. The objective of the task force would be to:

(i)   identify opportunities to align regional and country efforts on gender equality and to select the appropriate modality to progress action;

(ii)   refine indicators for the GMS-2030 results framework or develop a stand-alone regional gender results framework; and

(iii)   report to GMS ministers on progress and on any necessary actions required to improve regional efforts to accelerate gender equality.

90. The GMS Secretariat, GMS countries, and development partners could jointly define the corresponding scope of work and functions, members, and coordinating arrangements for the task force.

---

[29]   ADB. 2021. *Thematic Evaluation. ADB Support for the Greater Mekong Subregion Program, 2012-2020: Performance and Results.* Manila.

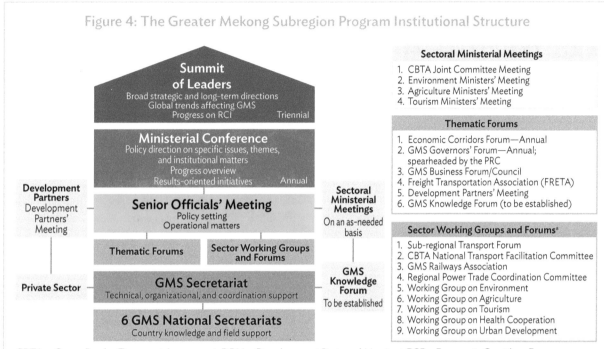

Figure 4: The Greater Mekong Subregion Program Institutional Structure

CBTA = Cross-Border Transport Agreement, DPM = Development Partners' Meeting, ECF = Economic Corridors Forum,
FRETA = Freight Transportation Group, GMS = Greater Mekong Subregion, PRC = People's Republic of China,
RCI = regional cooperation and integration.
a   In some cases, task forces are created for an interim period with the intention that they will be formalized into working groups
    in due course.
Source: The GMS Secretariat.

B. Capacity Building

91. As described above, policy dialogue is one of the key features of the GMS program. The diversity of the GMS countries, and their common shared geography and challenges, means policy discussions often deliver real benefit for GMS countries in terms of knowledge sharing and capacity building. Other forms of capacity building, such as twinning, coaching and mentoring, establishing scholarships, professional networks or communities of practice, as well as exploring policy support, will be explored as mechanisms to advance gender equality under the GMS Gender Strategy.

C. Knowledge Products

92. The institutional mechanisms of the GMS and its multi-tiered and sectoral specific bodies are important channels for the dissemination of advice, insights, and best practice experiences on improving gender

equality across the region. The GMS Secretariat will work with countries, including individual GMS countries as authors, and development partners to develop, or identify and share, knowledge products to help GMS countries and other stakeholders plan, execute, and evaluate gender interventions.

D. Pilot Projects

93. The GMS Program's well-established cooperative framework is the ideal steering mechanism for GMS countries, together or as a subset, to establish regional pilot projects to test the viability of innovative gender equality interventions. The GMS-2030 emphasizes an enhanced spatial approach, increased digitization in projects, and private sector engagement. The GMS Program will support the development of pilot initiatives projects to deploy new concepts and manage the risks of new technology and partnerships in particular areas of the GMS.

VI. Monitoring and Evaluation

A. Results Framework

94. A GMS results framework is being prepared by the GMS Secretariat to trace the implementation of GMS-2030 and its progress toward achieving the program's vision and mission. This will be supported by sector-specific results frameworks that will be developed by the respective GMS sector working groups.

95. Gender equality is identified as an integral cross-cutting theme in the GMS-2030, in recognition of the important role that economic cooperation has to play in advancing gender equality. Incorporating monitoring and evaluation of gender equality across the GMS program in the GMS-2030 results framework will demonstrate progress against agreed outputs and desired outcomes. It will move the gender activities of the GMS program beyond counting women in employment and their participation in consultations to actions that advance transformative and sustainable progress on gender equality. This approach acknowledges the complexity of advancing gender equality and will encourage greater gender mainstreaming and innovation in activities and project design.

96. To ensure that the gender equality dimension is implemented across all the sectors covered by the GMS-2030, it is proposed that gender indicators, outputs, and outcomes are included in the results framework for the GMS-2030 strategy, rather than in a separate evaluation document. Integration of gender equality within the broader results framework of the GMS-2030 Strategy will support effective integration of gender equality in all program activities.

97. Gender indicators, outputs, and outcomes can also be included in the strategic results frameworks for the GMS sector working groups.

98. This approach will embed gender equality as an element of the GMS Regional Investment Framework (RIF). Ensuring that gender equality is considered at the concept stage for individual projects, and that gender analysis, including the collection of sex-disaggregated statistics, occurs from the earliest design stage will avoid many of the challenges encountered by previous GMS programs.

B. Possible Indicators

99. At the country level, GMS countries are already monitoring their progress on advancing gender equality through the gender indicators contained in the SDGs. Progress is being reported on achievements under SDG 5 and under other SDGs, recognizing the cross-cutting nature of gender equality. For the GMS Gender Strategy to encourage full and equal participation in the benefits of regional cooperation, regardless of gender, and to add value to country efforts to accelerate gender equality, strategy activities should meet not only the objectives of the GMS-2030 but contribute to progress under the SDGs.

100. Including selected indicators from the SDGs in the GMS-2030 results framework will track regional cooperation towards the global goals, and at the same time assist in the alignment of individual GMS country efforts on gender equality for increased impact. The GMS gender assessment identified specific areas for action, including changing harmful social norms; preventing gender-based violence; increasing women's economic and social participation,

especially for marginalized groups; and strengthening data collection.

101.   Gender indicators in the GMS-2030 results framework will need to take into account the diversity of the GMS and the very different stages of economic and social development across the subregion. In some countries, participation in the formal labor market, including through unskilled jobs, will be a transformative and empowering achievement, while for others this will be achieved through participation in skilled employment and in STEM occupations. Access to child care could also be relevant in this context to enable participation in the labor market. The gender indicators could also encourage targets on gender-based violence, sexual exploitation and harassment at both a policy level and a capacity development level, and measurement of voice and agency.

102.   Together, the thematic areas of focus under the GMS-2030 pillars of community, connectivity, and competitiveness; the cross-cutting themes;

and the modalities of the GMS Program identify the action areas, entry points, and activities. The time frames for measuring progress under the GMS-2030 Strategy and the SDGs also align. This alignment also creates the potential for streamlining monitoring and reporting of activities under the GMS Gender Strategy and the SDGs. The strategy will then be an important tool supporting increased gender data collection and capacity building across the subregion.

103.   Supporting capacity building in the collection and analysis of gender data—to increase the consistency in data collection across the subregion as identified in the GMS gender assessment—will underpin the GMS results framework. For some countries, developing data collection systems covering remote or regional areas will remain a challenge since they do not have a significant digital infrastructure. The GMS Gender Strategy work on gender indicators can add further evidence for digital investments in those areas, to support greater inclusion.

Appendix: Possible Gender Indicators

Impact	Gender equality accelerated across the GMS through activities to increase community, connectivity, and competitiveness	
Outcome	Share the benefits of regional cooperation more broadly	
	Action and Activity	**Indicators**
1	**Support GMS countries to improve the availability of sex-disaggregated data related to the Sustainable Development Goals**	
	All GMS countries have gaps in the data needed to report on the gender indicators in the Sustainable Development Goals.[a]	(i) Number of GMS programs, activities and initiatives that support sex-disaggregated data collection for the gender equality indicators in the UN Sustainable Development Goals
2	Elevate action on gender-based violence[b]	
	The GMS program is committed to including measures on gender-based violence prevention and response, including trafficking in people, in its programs, projects and activities.	(i) Proportion of new GMS projects that incorporate gender-based violence education and prevention activities (ii) Number of GMS activities annually that include gender-based violence legal and policy response capacity building
3	**Support shifting social norms that limit women's full participation in economic and social activities[c]**	
	Changing norms and attitudes concerned with entrenched gender roles and responsibilities is a long-term activity. The GMS Program can support changes to social norms and attitudes on gender equality by reducing gender gaps in (i) women's labor force participation, (ii) women's leadership, (iii) employment in non-traditional areas, and (iv) women's access to health care.	(i) Percentage of new projects with female employment targets (ii) Percentage of completed projects that met female employment targets (iii) Percentage of projects and activities that support training for women in entrepreneurial/ business skills (iv) Number of annual women's leadership events on including women in public life (v) Percentage of GMS meetings and workshops that incorporate proactive measures to advance gender equality[d] (vi) Number of gender-responsive and inclusive GMS projects supporting women and/or men in non-traditional employment[e] (vii) Progress in key health indicators

continued on next page

Appendix *continued*

		Action and Activity	Indicators
4		**Reduce gender inequality within and among countries**[f]	
		Women from ethnic minorities and women with disabilities are some of the poorest and most vulnerable groups in the GMS. The GMS program will support projects and activities that promote social and economic inclusion of these groups.	(i) Number of GMS projects and activities that actively support social and economic inclusion of women from ethnic minorities and women with disabilities (ii) Number of events or awareness campaigns promoting women from ethnic minorities and women with disabilities

GMS = Greater Mekong Subregion, Lao PDR = Lao People's Democratic Republic, SDG = Sustainable Development Goal, UN = United Nations.

[a] As of December 2020, countries had the following proportion of indicators in place to monitor the SDGs from a gender perspective: Cambodia (56.5%), People's Republic of China (22.1%), Lao PDR (37.7%), Myanmar (44.3%), Thailand (45.9%), and Viet Nam (41.9%).

[b] Relates to SDG indicators: SDG 5.2.1, 5.2.2, 11.7.2, and 16.2.3.

[c] Relates to SDG indicators: SDG 2.3.2, 5.4.2, 5.5.2, 8.3.1, 8.5.1, 8.5.2, 8.7.1, 8.8.1, 16.2.2, 16.7.1, and 16.7.2.

[d] This could include achieving a gender balance of speakers for conferences and knowledge events, gender thematic activities, provision of child care for participants, and family-friendly hours.

[e] Gender-responsive means that training, scholarship and internship opportunities take into account the different needs and challenges faced by men and women.

[f] Relates to SDG indicators: SDG 1.1.1, 1.2.1, 5.a and 5b, and 10.2.1

Source: UN Women. 2022. Country Fact Sheets.

Bibliography

23rd GMS Ministerial Conference, Phnom Penh 2019. *The Greater Mekong Subregion Economic Cooperation Program Strategic Framework 2030.*

Australian Centre for International Agricultural Research. Gender Equitable Agricultural Extension Through Institutions and Youth Engagement in Papua New Guinea. Canberra.

Australian Centre for International Agricultural Research. Analysing Gender Transformative Approaches to Agricultural Development with Ethnic Minority Communities in Vietnam. Canberra.

ASEAN and UN Women. 2021. *ASEAN Gender Outlook : Achieving the SDGs for All and Leaving No Woman or Girl Behind.* Jakarta and Bangkok.

Asian Development Bank (ADB). 2000. *Gender Checklist: Agriculture.* Manila.

ADB. 2006. *Gender Checklist: Health.* Manila.

ADB. 2006. *Gender Checklist: Urban Development and Housing.* Manila.

ADB. 2006. *Gender Checklist: Water Supply and Sanitation.* Manila.

ADB. 2012. *Gender Tool Kit: Energy Going Beyond the Meter.* Manila.

ADB. 2013. *Toolkit on Gender Equality Results and Indicators.* Manila.

ADB. 2013. *Gender Tool Kit: Transport—Maximizing the Benefits of Improved Mobility for All.* Manila.

Boniol, M. et al. 2019. Gender Equity in the Health Workforce: Analysis of 104 Countries. *Health Workforce Working Paper* 1. Geneva: World Health Organization. March.

Carvalho, R. and E. Lopez. 2020. Coronavirus: Asian Women Pay the Price of Pandemic As COVID-19 Ravages Economies, Jobs. *South China Morning Post.* 12 December.

Government of Australia, Department of Foreign Affairs and Trade. 2020. *Partnerships for Recovery—Australia's COVID-19 Development Response.* Canberra.

GIZ. Regional Economic Development Program IV.

Henson, S. 2018. *Gender and Sanitary and Phytosanitary Measures in the Context of Trade: A Review of Issues and Policy Recommendations.* Geneva: International Centre for Trade and Sustainable Development.

Hill, E. and M. Baird. 2020. COVID-19, Economic Crisis and Gender Equality in Asia. *East Asia Forum.* 10 June.

Elborgh-Woytek, K. et al. 2013. *Women, Work, and the Economy: Macroeconomic Gains From Gender Equity.* IMF Staff Discussion Note. International Monetary Fund. September.

Krainara, C. 2013. Cross Border Trade Outlook in the GMS. March.

Madgavkar, A. et al. 2020. *COVID-19 and Gender Equality: Countering the Regressive Effects.* McKinsey Global Institute. 15 July.

United Nations (UN). Office of the United Nations High Commissioner for Human Rights 2012. *Born Free and Equal: Sexual Orientation, Gender Identity and Sex Characteristics in International Human Rights Law*. Geneva.

United Nations Framework Convention on Climate Change. Introduction to Gender and Climate Change.

UN Secretary-General's High-Level Panel on Women's Economic Empowerment. 2017. Driver 1 Working Group Paper: Changing Norms in Support of Women's Economic Empowerment.

UN Women. 2021. *Progress on the Sustainable Development Goals: The Gender Snapshot 2021*. New York.

UN Women. Policy Brief No. 4. Why Macroeconomic Policy Matters for Gender Equality. New York.

Woetze, J. et al. 2018. *The Power of Parity: Advancing Women's Equality in Asia Pacific*. McKinsey Global Institute. 23 April.

Women's World Banking. 2015. *Access to Finance of Women-Owned SMEs in Southeast Asia: An Assessment of Five Countries*.

World Bank. 2012. *Fostering Women's Economic Empowerment Through Special Economic Zones*. Washington, DC.

World Bank. 2018. *Addressing Gender-Based Violence in Investment Project Financing Involving Major Civil Work*. Washington, DC.

World Bank. 2020. *Gender-Inclusive Cities: Can Urban Planning Take Into Account Women and Minorities?* Washington, DC.

World Bank. 2020. *Good Practice Notes: Addressing Sexual Exploitation and Abuse and Sexual Harassment (SEA/SH) in Investment Project Financing Involving Major Civil Works*. Washington, DC.

CPSIA information can be obtained
at www.ICGtesting.com
Printed in the USA
JSHW070942160523
41776JS00006B/173